W9-BKY-740

SHIRLEY VALENTINE

A Play by

WILLY RUSSELL

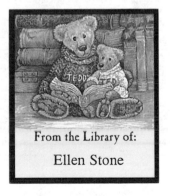

From the Library of:

Ellen Stone

Copyright © 1988, 1989 by W.R. Limited

ALL RIGHTS RESERVED

CAUTION: *Professionals and amateurs are hereby warned that SHIRLEY VALENTINE is subject to a royalty. It is fully protected under the copyright laws of the United States of America, the British Commonwealth, including Canada, and all other countries of the Copyright Union. All rights, including professional, amateur, motion pictures, recitation, lecturing, public reading, radio broadcasting, television, and the rights of translation into foreign languages are strictly reserved. In its present form the play is dedicated to the reading public only.*

The amateur live stage performance rights to SHIRLEY VALENTINE are controlled exclusively by Samuel French, Inc., and royalty arrangements and licenses must be secured well in advance of presentation. PLEASE NOTE *that amateur royalty fees are set upon application in accordance with your producing circumstances. When applying for a royalty quotation and license please give us the number of performances intended, dates of production, your seating capacity and admission fee. Royalties are payable one week before the opening performance of the play to Samuel French, Inc., at 45 West 25th Street, New York, NY 10010; or at 7623 Sunset Blvd., Hollywood CA 90046, or to Samuel French (Canada), Ltd., 100 Lombard Street, Toronto, Ontario, Canada M5C 1M3.*

Royalty of the required amount must be paid whether the play is presented for charity or gain and whether or not admission is charged.

Stock royalty quoted on application to Samuel French, Inc.

For all other rights other than those stipulated above, apply to Casarotto Ramsay, Ltd., 60 Wardour St., London W1V 3HP.

Particular emphasis is laid on the question of amateur or professional readings, permission and terms for which must be secured in writing from Samuel French, Inc.

Copying from this book on whole or in print is strictly forbidden by law, and the right of performance is not transferable.

Whenever the play is produced the following notice must appear on all programs, printing and advertising for the play: "Produced by special arrangement with Samuel French, Inc."

Due authorship credit must be given on all programs, printing and advertising for the play.

ISBN 0 573 69120 7   Printed in U.S.A.

IMPORTANT BILLING AND CREDIT REQUIREMENTS

All producers of SHIRLEY VALENTINE *must* give credit to the Author of the Play in all programs distributed in connection with performances of the Play and in all instances in which the title of the Play appears for purposes of advertising, publicizing or otherwise exploiting the Play and/or a production. The name of the Author *must* also appear on a separate line, in which no other name appears, immediately following the title, and *must* appear in size of type not less than fifty percent the size of the title type.

Anyone presenting the play shall not commit or authorize any act or omission by which the copyright of the play or the right to copyright same may be impaired.

No changes shall be made in the play for the purpose of your production.
The publication of this play does not imply that it is necessarily available for performance by amateurs or professionals. Amateurs and professionals considering a production are strongly advised in their own interests to apply to Samuel French, Inc., for consent before starting rehearsals, advertising, or booking a theatre or hall.

No part of this book may be reproduced, stored in a retrieval system, or transmitted in any form, by any means, including mechanical, electronic, photocopying, recording, videotaping, or otherwise, without the prior written permission of the publisher.

SHIRLEY VALENTINE

Inside Mrs. Joe Bradshaw -- 42 year-old mother of two grown children -- is the former Shirley Valentine longing to get out. Her hope and self-confidence badly shattered by school, marriage and life, she is reduced to talking to the kitchen wall whilst preparing her husband's evening meal -- to be on the table as he opens the front door every night. As she sips a glass of wine she dreams of drinking in a country where the grape is grown. Her feminist friend offers her a holiday in Greece and, with great trepidation and a lot of forward planning, Shirley seizes the opportunity and goes, to enounter a totally different lifestyle. Shirley, breaking out of the mould cast for her by society, is brilliantly shown with humour, warm sympathy and human insight by the author of *Educating Rita* and *Blood Brothers*.

SHIRLEY VALENTINE

First presented in London by Bob Swash at the
Vaudeville Theatre on 21st January, 1988 with the
following cast:

Shirley   Pauline Collins

Directed by Simon Callow
Designed by Bruno Santini

SHIRLEY VALENTINE

by Willy Russell

First presented in New York City by The Really Useful
Theatre Company, Inc. and Bob Swash at The Booth
Theatre, a Shubert Organization Theatre, Gerald
Schoenfeld, Chairman, Bernard B. Jacobs, President, on
February 16, 1989 with the following cast:

Shirley............Pauline Collins

Directed by Simon Callow
Designed by Bruno Santini
Lighting by Nick Chelton

Originally produced in London by Bob Swash

Pauline Collins is appearing with the permission of
Actors' Equity Association under an exchange program
between American Equity and British Equity.
The Producers wish to express their appreciation to
Theatre Development Fund for its support of this
production.

STANDBYS
Standbys never substitute for listed players unless a specific
announcement for the appearance is made at the time of the
performance..
Standby for Miss Collins -- Patricia Kilgarriff.

SYNOPSIS OF SCENES

ACT I, Scene 1 The kitchen of a semi-detached
house. Evening
ACT I, Scene 2 The same. Three weeks later

ACT II, A Greek island

SHIRLEY VALENTINE

ACT I

SCENE 1

(The kitchen of a semi-detached house. It is a well established kitchen, bearing signs of additions and alterations which have been made over the years. It is not a highly personalized palace of pitch pine and hanging baskets but nevertheless has signs of personality having overcome the bleakness of chipboard and formica. It is quite a comfortable and reassuring place. Specifically the kitchen contains--apart from the obvious cooker, fridge etc.--a door which leads out of the house, a wall with a window, a dining-table and chairs. As the curtain rises SHIRLEY is beginning preparations for cooking the evening meal--this includes opening a bottle of wine from which she pours a glass. Throughout the following scene she sets a table for two, as she prepares, cooks and finally serves one of the truly great but unsung dishes of world cuisine--chips and egg.)

SHIRLEY. Y'know I like a glass of wine when I'm doin the cookin'. Don't I, wall? Don't I like a glass of wine when I'm preparing the evening meal? Chips an'egg! *(She takes a sip of wine.)* I never used to drink wine. It was our Millandra who started me on this. She said to me, she said, "Mother! Mother, nobody drinks rum an' coke these days. Everybody drinks wine now. Oh Mother! Have a glass of Riesling instead." Kids. They know everything, don't they? Our Millandra was goin' through her slightly intellectual phase at the time. Y'know her, an' her mate--Sharron-Louise. Because it was all white wine an' Bruce Springsteen at the time. Y'know the pair of them stopped goin' down the clubs in town an' started hangin' out in that bistro all the time. Y'know, where the artists and the poets go. They seen, erm, what's-his-name one night, erm, Henry Adrian, yeh. Apparently Sharron-Louise got his autograph. And breakfast as well, I believe. Anyway, the pair of them are out of that phase now. And am I glad. Because y'know the two of them'd sit at the table for hours an' all's you'd hear from the pair of them was--"It was great. It was great. Was a laugh, wasn't it? " Then they'd both go back into trance for half an hour an' you'd suddenly hear--"It was brilliant last night. It was more than brillant. It was mega brill." Yeh, it was, it was double fab, wasn't it?" And d' y' know, no matter how long they sat there, you'd never get to know what it was that was so

double fab an' mega brill. *(pause)* Maybe it was
the breakfasts! Mind you, I do miss them, the
kids. Our Millandra shares a flat with Sharron-
Louise now. An' our Brian's livin' in a squat. In
Kirkby. I said to him, I said, "Brian, if you're
gonna live in a squat, son, couldn't y' pick
somewhere nice. Y'know, somewhere like
Childwall?" "Mother, he said to me, "Childwall
is no place for a poet." 'Cos that's our Brian's
latest scheme. This one is--he's become Britain's
latest first-ever busker poet. What's he like, wall?
The language. "I hate the fuckin' daffodils/I hate
the blue remembered hills." He's loop the loop.
Mind you, I'm glad he's given up archery. Oh
God, look at the time. What am I doin' sittin' here
talkin' and *he'll* be in for his tea, won't he. An'
what's he like? My feller. What's he like, wall?
Well, he likes everything to be as it's always
been. Like his tea always has to be on the table as
he comes through that door. If the plate isn't
landin' the table just as his foot is landin' on the
mat, there's ructions. I've given up arguin'. I
said to him, once, I said, "Listen, Joe. If your tea
isn't on the table at the same time every night it
doesn't mean that the pound's collapsed y'know,
or that there's been a world disaster. All it means,
Joe, is that one of the billions of human bein's on
this planet has to eat his tea at a different time."
Well, did it do any good? I could've been talkin' to
that. Couldn't I, wall? I could have been talkin' to
you. *(pause)* I always said I'd leave him when the

kids grew up. But by the time they'd grown up there was nowhere to go. Well, you don't start again at forty-two, do y'? They say, don't they, they say once you've reached your forties life gets a bit jaded an' y' start to believe that the only good things are things in the past. Well, I must have been an early developer, I felt like that at twenty-five. I'm not sayin' he's bad, my feller. He's just no bleedin' good. Mind you, I think most of them are the same, aren't they? I mean they're lovely at first. Know, when they're courtin' y'. Y'know, before you've had the horizontal party with them, oh they're marvellous then. They'll do anything for y'. Nothin' is too much trouble. But the minute, the very minute, after they've first had y'--their behaviour starts to change. It's like that advert, isn't it? I was watchin' it it the other night y' know, Cadburys' Milk Tray Man. Oh, he's marvellous, isn't he? Y'see him, he dives off a thousand foot cliff an' swims across two miles of water, just to drop off a box of Cadburys' chocolates. An' y' learn from that that the lady loves Milk Tray. And that the lady's been keepin' her legs firmly closed. Because if she hadn't, if he'd had his way with her he wouldn't go there by divin' off a thousand foot cliff an' swimmin' through a ragin' torrent. He'd go by bus. An' there'd be no chocolates. If she mentioned the chocolates that he used to bring he'd say "Oh no Babe. I've stopped bringin' y' chocolates, 'cos y' puttin' a bit too much weight on." D' y' know,

when y' think about it, Cadbury's could go out of
business if women didn't hold back a bit. I don't
hate men. I'm not a feminist. Not like Jane.
Jane's my mate. Now, she's a feminist. Well, she
likes to think she is, y' know she reads
Cosmopolitan an' says that all men are potential
rapists. Even the Pope. Well, Jane does hate men.
She divorced her husband, y' know. I never knew
him, it was before I met Jane. Apparently she
came back from work one mornin' an' found her
husband in bed with the milkman. With the
milkman, honest to God! Well, apparently, from
that day forward Jane was a feminist. An' I've
noticed, she never takes milk in her tea. I haven't
known Jane all that long, be she's great. She's
goin' to Greece for a fortnight. Next month she's
goin' God, what will I do for two weeks? She's the
only one who keeps me sane. Jane's the only one I
ever talk to, apart from the wall--isn't she, wall?
She is. I said to her this mornin', "Jane, I won't
half miss y'". You know what she said to me? "I
want you to come with me." (*She laughs.*) Silly
bitch. Hey, wall, wall, imagine the face on
"him". Imagine the face if he had to look after
himself for two weeks. Jesus, if I go to the
bathroom for five minutes he thinks I've been
hijacked. (*She takes a sip of wine.*) Oh, it's
lovely, that. It's not too dry. Some of it'd strip the
palate off y', wouldn't it? But this is lovely. (*She
takes another sip and savours it.*) It's nice. Wine.
It's like it's been kissed by the sun. "He" doesn't

drink wine. "he" says wine is nothin' but a posh way of gettin' pissed. I suppose it is really. But it's nice. Know what I'd like to do, I'd like to drink a glass of wine in a country where the grape is grown. Sittin' by the sea. Lookin' at the sun. But "he" won't go abroad. Well, y' see, he gets jet lag when we go to the Isle of Man. An' I wouldn't mine--we go by boat. We've been goin' there for fifteen years--he still won't drink the tap water. He's that type, Joe. Gets culture shock if we go to Chester. See, what Jane says is, he's entitled to his own mind an' that's fine. If he doesn't wanna go abroad, well that's up to him. But that shouldn't stop me goin'. If I want to. An' I know Jane's right. I know. It's logical. Dead logical. But like I said to her, "Jane, y' can't bring logic into this-- we're talkin' about marriage. "Marriage is like the Middle East, isn't it? There 's no solution. You jiggle things around a bit, give up a bit here, take a bit there, deal with the flare-ups when they happen. But most of the time you just keep your head down, observe the curfew and hope that the cease-fire holds. (*pause*) 'Course, that was when Jane handed me the time bomb. She's only gone an' paid for me to go, hasn't she? She handed me the tickets this morning'. (*She goes to her bag and produces an air ticket from which she reads.*) "Bradshaw. S. Mrs. BD. Five-eight-one. Twenty- third of June. Nineteen hundred. From Man. to Cor." Jane said she didn't want to go on her own. She'd just got the money through from the sale of their house. Well, how the hell could I tell her it was impossible? I'll give her the tickets back tomorrow. She'll easily find someone else to go with her. I shouldn't have taken the bloody tickets off her in the first place. Well, I tried to like, tried to expl...to tell her it was impossible. But y' know what feminists are like. If something's impossible, that's the perfect reason for doin' it. Hey, wall, it'd be fantastic though, wouldn't it? I just lay his tea in front of him an' I turn away all dead cas, an' say "Oh, by the way, babe--I'm just poppin' off to Greece for a fortnight. Yeh. I just thought I'd mention it so's y' can put it in y' diary. You won't mind doin' y' own washin' and cookin' for a couple of weeks, will y'? There's nothing to it, doll. The white blob on the left of the kitchen is the washin' machine an' the brown blob on the right is the cooker. An' don't get them mixed up, will y' or y' might end up with socks on toast." Some chance, eh wall? Some chance. (*She returns the ticket to her bag.*) Y'know, if I said to him...if I said I was off to Greece for a fortnight, he'd think it was for the sex. Wouldn't he, wall? Well...two women, on their own, goin' to Greece. Well, it's obvious, isn't it? I wouldn't mind I'm not even particularly fond of it--sex--am I, wall? I'm not. I think sex is like Sainsbury's--y' know, overrated. It's just a lot of pushin' an' shovin' an' y' still come out with very little in the end. 'Course it would've been different if I'd been born into the next generation, our Millandra's generation. 'Cos it's different for them, isn't it? They discovered it, y'see, the clitoris. The Clitoris Kids, I call them. And good luck to them, I don't begrudge them anythin'. But when I was a girl we'd never heard of this clitoris. In those days everyone thought it was just a case of "in out, in out, shake it all about", stars'd light up the sky an' the earth would tremble. The only thing that trembled for me was the headboard on the bed. But y'see, the clitoris hadn't been discovered then, had it? I mean, obviously, it was always there, like penicillin, an' America. It was there but it's not really there until it's been discovered, is it? Maybe I should have married Christoper Columbus! I was about, about twenty-eight when I first read all about it, the clitoris. It was dead interestin'. Apparently it was all Freud's fault. Y' know, Sigmund. You see, what happened was, Freud had said that there were two ways for a woman to have an orgasm. An' the main one could only be caused by havin' the muscles, inside, stimulated. An' the other, orgasm, it was supposed to be like an inferior, second-rate one, was caused by the little clitoris. Now y' see, that's what Freud had said. An' everyone had believed him. Well, you would, wouldn't y'? I mean, Sigmund Freud, who's gonna argue with Sigmund Freud. I mean, say you're just--just standin' at the bus stop, you an' Sigmund Freud, the bus comes along, y' say to him "Does this bus go to Fazakerley?" He nods an' says to y', "Yes,

this is one of the buses that goes to Fazakerley."
Well, you'd get on the bus, wouldn't you? But I'll
tell y' what--you'd be bloody lucky if y' ever
reached Fazakerley. Because there's only *one* bus
that goes to Fazakerley. The clitoris bus. The
other bus doesn't go anywhere near Fazakerley.
But y' see, everyone believed him an' they've been
giving out wrong information for years, y' know
like they did with spinach. It's marvellous, isn't
it--tellin' people there's two kinds of orgasm. It's
like tellin' people there's two Mount Everests--
some people stumble on to the real mountain while
the rest of us are all runnin'up this little hillock
an' wonderin' why the view's not very good when
we get to the top. Well when I first read about all
this I was fascinated, wasn't I, wall? But y' know
when you read a word for the first time an' you've
never heard it spoken, you can get it wrong, can't
y'? 'Know, pronounce it wrong. Like, when I was
little there was a kid in our street called Gooey.
Honest. Gooey. His mother used to go, "Gooey. Y'
tea's ready, Gooey. Come on in, Gooey." Well, y'
see, when she'd been lookin' for a name for him
she'd been readin' this American magazine an'
she saw this name, G.U.Y. Guy. But she thought it
was pronounced Gooey. So that's what she
christened him. Gooey McFadden, he was called.
Well, it was the same with the clitoris. When I
first read the word I thought it was pronounced
clit*or*is. I still think it sounds nicer that way,
actually. Clit*or*is. That even sounds like it could

be a name, doesn't it? Clitoris. "Oh, hi-ya
Clitoris, how are y'? Oh, really. Listen Clitoris,
wait till I tell y'..." (*She thinks about it.*) Oh, shut
up, wall. I think it sounds nice. Why not? There's
plenty of men walkin' round called "Dick".
Well, anyway, that's how I thought it was
pronounced when I first mentioned it to Joe. We
were sittin' in the front room an' I said, "Joey.
Joe, have you ever heard about the clitoris?. He
didn't even look up from his paper. "Yeh", he
said, "but it doesn't go as well as the Ford
Cortina."

(*pause*)

Wait till he finds out he's gettin' chips an' egg for
his tea tonight. Well, its Thursday, isn't it? And
on Thursday it has to be steak. It's the eleventh
commandment, isn't it? Moses declared it. "Thou
shalt give they feller steak every Thursday and if
thou doesn't, thy feller will have one big gob on
him all night long." What will he be like, wall?
What will he be like when he sees it's only chips
an' egg? An' I wouldn't mind, it's not even my
bloody fault about the steak. Well, I gave it the
dog, y'see. This dog at the place I work. Well it's
a bloodhound, y'see. But this couple I work for--
they're vegans. Y' know, the vegetarian lunatic
fringe--the Marmite Tendency I call them. Well,
they've brought up this bloodhound as a
vegetarian. Well, it's not natural, is it? I mean, if

God had wanted to create it as a vegetarian dog he wouldn't have created it as a bloodhound, would he? He would have made it as a grapejuice hound. But this dog is a bloodhound. It needs meat. Well, it was just on impulse, really. I'm there, today, an' I looked at this dog an' all's I could think about was the pound an' a half of best steak that's in me bag. Well, d' y' know, I think it was worth what I'll have to put up with from "him" tonight; just to see the look on that dog's face as it tasted meat from the first time. 'Course, I don't think Joe'd quite see it that way. "Y' did what? What did y' do? Y' give it to the dog? You've gone bloody mental, woman. Is this it? Have y' finally gone round the pipe?" (*She adopts a rather grand gesture and voice.*) "Yes, Joseph, I rather think I have. I have finally gone loop the facking loop. I have become crazy with joy, because today Jane gave me the opportunity of getting away for a fortnight. Joe! I am to travel to Greece with my companion. Our departure is less than three weeks hence and we shall be vacationing for some fourteen days. And now I must away, leaving you to savour your chips and your Chuckie egg whilst I supervise the packing of my trunk." (*She drops the pose.*) Our Brian was. round before. I showed him the tickets. Didn't I, wall? An' what did he say? "Mother, just go. Forget about me father, forget about everythin', just get yourself on the plane an' go." (*She laughs.*) Well, that's how he is, our Brian; you

wanna do somethin', you just do it. Bugger the
consequences. He's a nutcase. But he couldn't
care less. An' he's always been the same. He was
like that when he was a little kid, when he was at
school. Hey, wall remember the nativity play? Oh
God. Our Brian was only about eight or nine an'
the school had given up with him. The teachers
just said he was loop the loop an' that was that. I
agreed with them. But the headmaster, the
headmaster was fascinated by our Brian. He like,
like studied him. He said to me, "There's no
malice in the child, no malice whatsoever but it
would appear that Brian has no concept of
consequences. I think what we have to do with
Brian is to try and give him more responsibility
and so I've decided to give him the star part in the
nativity play this year." Well, when Brian
learned he'd got the part of Joseph he was made up
with himself. Ah, God love him, he thought he'd
been picked 'cos he was great at actin' an' I
couldn't say anythin' because it was workin', y'
see, this psychology. All the time he's rehearsin'
this nativity play his behaviour is fantastic; the
headmaster's made up with him. I'm made up
with him, the teachers are made up with him. An'
he's made up with himself. He's practisin', every
night in his room--(*on one note*) "We are weary
travellers on our way to Bethlehem an' my wife is
having a baby and we need rest at the inn for the
night." Well, the day of the show, I got down to the
school, the play started an' it was lovely, y' know,

all the little angels come on an' they all have a sly little wave to their mams. Then it was our Brian's entrance; he comes on an' he's pullin' this donkey behind him--it's like this hobby-horse on wheels. An' perched on top of it is this little girl, takin' the part of the Virgin Mary an' she's dressed beautiful, y' know, her mother's really dolled her up to be the part. An' she's givin' a little wave to her mam. So Brian gives the donkey a bit of a tug because he's takin' it dead serious an' he doesn't believe they should be wavin' to their mams. He's up there, he's actin' like he might win the Oscar--y' know, he's mimin' givin' hay to the donkey an' he's pattin' it on the head. Well, the headmaster turned round an' smiled at me. I think he was as proud of our Brian as I was. Well, Brian gets to the door of the inn and he goes "Knock, knock, knock" an' the little Innkeeper appears. Our Brian starts "We are weary travellers on our way to Bethlehem an' my wife is havin' a baby an' we need to rest for the night at the inn." So the little feller playin' the Innkeeper pipes up: "You cannot stay at the inn because the inn is full up an' there is no room in the inn." An' then our Brain is supposed to say somethin' like: "Well, we must go an' find a lowly cattle shed an' stay in there." Then he's supposed to go off pullin' the donkey an' the Virgin Mary behind him. But he didn't. Well, I don't know if it's the Virgin Mary, gettin' up our Brian's nose, because she's spent the whole scene wavin' to her mother, or whether it was just that our Brian suddenly realized that the part of Joseph wasn't as big as it had been cracked up to be. But whatever it was, instead of goin' off pullin' the donkey, he suddenly turned to the little Innkeeper an' yelled at him: "Full up? Full up? But we booked!" Well, the poor little Innkeeper didn't know what day of the week it was. He's lookin' all round the hall for someone to rescue him an' his bottom lip's beginnin' to tremble an' our Brian's goin', "Full up? I've got the wife outside, waitin' with the donkey. She's expectin' a baby any minute now, there's snow everywhere in six-foot drifts an' you're tryin' to tell me that you're full up?" Well, the top brass on the front row are beginn' to look a bit uncomfortable--they're beginnin' to turn and look at the headmaster an' our Brian's givin' a perfect imitation of his father, on a bad day; he's beratin' anythin' that dares move. The little Innkeeper's lip is goin' ten to the dozen, the Virgin Mary's in floods of tears on the donkey an' one of the three Wise Men has started to wet himself. Well, the Innkeeper finally grasps that the script is well out of the window an' that he has to do somethin' about our Brian. So he steps forward an' he says, "Listen, mate, listen! I was only jokin'. We have got room really. Y' can come in if y' want. An' with that the three of them disappeared into the inn. End of nativity play an' end of our Brian's actin' career. Me an' our Brian, we sometimes have a laugh about it now, but at the time I could have died of shame. It was all over the papers: "Mary And Joseph Fail To Arrive in Bethlehem." I was ashamed. (*pause*) It's no wonder really, that I've never travelled anywhere meself; it must be God punishin' me for raisin' a child who managed to prevent Mary an' Joseph reachin' their destination. An' there was me when I was a girl--the only thing I ever wanted to do was travel. I always wanted to be a-- courier. Or an air hostess. But it was only the clever ones who got to do things like that. When I got my final report from school the headmistress had written at the bottom of it: "I can confidently predict that Miss Valentine"--that was me maiden name--"I can confidently predict that Miss Valentine will not go far in life. I feel this is just as well for, given her marks in geography, she would surely get lost." She was a mare, that headmistress. She used to come into assembly sometimes an' ask like a spot question, an' whoever got it right would get loads of house-points, an' it was nearly always Marjorie Majors who got it right--she took private elocution lessons an' she left school with just under four billion house-points. One day, we were all standin' there in assembly an' this headmistress appeared; " A question," she said to everyone, "a question: what was man's most important invention?" Well, every hand in the hall shot up. "Me, miss", "I know, miss", "Miss, miss, me, miss". An' my hand was up with the rest of them because for once

I knew the answer. But this headmistress, she took one look at me an' said, "Oh, put your hand down, Shirley, you won't know the answer", an' she started goin' round the hall, the grin on her face gettin' smugger an' smugger as she got answers like, "the sputnik", "the cathode ray tube", "the automatic washin' machine". Even the clever ones were gettin' it wrong--even Marjorie Majors. But I kept my arm up there in the air because I knew I had the right answer. I'd got it from me dad, an' he'd got it from the *Encyclopaedia Britannica.* Ah, y' know me dad, he was still goin' on about that *Encyclopaedia Britannica* when he was on his death-bed. "How can those kids of mine be so thick when I bought them the *Encyclopaedia Britannica?*" He got a lot of pleasure out of it, though. He'd sit there for hours readin' it an' he'd try to impress us all with these dead odd facts. An' I'd remembered him sayin' about man's most important invention because it was so ordinary. So I'm stood there in assembly, me arm stuck up in the air, an' I'm like the cat with the cream because this headmistress has done the length an' breadth of the hall an' still no-one's come up with the right answer. Well, I'm the only one left so she turns to me an' she says, "All right then, Shirley, come on, you might as well get it wrong along with everyone else. Do you remember the question, Shirley--what was man's most important invention?" Well, I paused, y'know, savourin'

the moment, knowin' I was on the brink of
receivin' at least forty-three thousand house-
points an' a blessin' from the Pope. But when I
said, "the wheel", it was like this headmistress
had been shot in the back. I thought maybe she
hadn't heard me squeaky little voice so I said it
again, louder: "The wheel, miss. Man's most
important invention was--" But I never got to
finish because I was cut off by this scream from
the headmistress. "*You*", she yelled, "you must
have been told that answer!" I just stood there,
reelin' with shock. An' I tried to ask her, to say--
to say, how--how the bloody hell else was I
supposed to know the right answer? But she
wouldn't listen. She just ignored me an' told the
demented music teacher to get on with playin' the
hymn. An' all me house-points, an' me blessin'
from the Pope, just disappeared before me eyes as
she led the hall into singin' " Glad That I Live
Am I". I was never really interested in school
after that. I became a rebel. I wore me school skirt
so high y' wouldv'e thought it was a serviette. I
was marvellous. I used to have the chewy goin' all
day, like that...(*She chews*.)...an' I'd just exude
boredom out of every pore. I hated everythin'.
"Oh, I hate him", "Oh I hate her", "I hate this, I
hate that". It's garbage", "It's last", "It's crap".
"I hate it." But I didn't hate anythin', y'know.
The only thing I hated was me. I didn't want to be
a rebel. I wanted to be nice. I wanted to be like
Marjorie Majors. I used to pick on her somethin'

rotten an' I really wanted to be like her. Can't y' be evil when you're a kid? I saw her a few weeks ago, Marjorie Majors. Didn't I, wall? I hadn't even heard of her for years. I'm in town, loaded down with shoppin', an' what's the first thing that always happens when y' in town loaded with shoppin'? Right. The heavens opened. An' it's funny the way all these things are linked but they are; once you're in town, loaded with shoppin' bags, caught in a deluge--it always follows that every bus ever made disappears off the face of the earth. Well, I' standin' there, like a drowned rat, me hair's in ruins an' I've got mascara lines runnin' from me face to me feet, so I thought I might as well trudge up to the *Adelphi* an' get a taxi. "Course, when I got there the taxis had gone into hidin' along with the buses. Well, I'm just rootin' in me bag, lookin' for somethin' to slash me wrists with then this big white car pulls up to the hotel an', of course, I'm standin' right by a puddle an' as the wheels go through it, half the puddle ends up over me an' the other half in me shoppin' bags. Well, all I wanted to do by this time was scream. So I did. I just opened me mouth, standin' there in front of the hotel an' let out this scream. I could've been arrested but I didn't care. Well, I was in mid-scream when I noticed this woman get out the white car an' start comin' towards me. An' she's dead elegant. Y'know, she's walkin' through this torrential rain an' I guarantee not one drop of it was landin' on her.

But the second she opened her mouth I knew who
she was. I'd recognize those elocution lessons
anywhere. "Forgive me for asking," she said,
"but didn't you used to be Shirley Valentine?" I
just stood there, starin'. And drippin'. "It is," she
said, "it's Shirley." An' the next thing, she's
apologizin' for half drownin' me an' she's
pullin' me into the hotel an' across the lobby an'
into this lounge that's the size of two football
pitches. Well, she's ordered tea an' I'm sittin'
there, rain water drippin' down me neck an'
plastic carrier bags round me feet, an' I'm
thinkin', "Well Marjorie, you've waited a long
time for your revenge but you've got me good style
now, haven't y'? Well, go on, spare me the torture,
just put the knife in quick an' let's get it over
with; come on, tell me all about you bein' an air
hostess on Concorde." But she didn't say
anythin'. She just sat there, lookin' at me, y'
know, really lookin' at me. I thought I'm not
gonna let her milk it so I said, "You're an air
hostess these days, aren't y', Marjorie? Oh yes, I
hear it's marvellous. You travel all over the
world, don't you?" But she still just kept on
lookin' at me. The waitress was just puttin' the
tea an' cakes on the table in front of us, I said to
her: "This is my friend Marjorie. We were at
school together. Marjorie's an air hostess." "An
air hostess?" Marjorie suddenly said, "Darling,
whatever gave you that idea? I certainly travel
widely but I'm not an air hostess. Shirley, I'm a

hooker. A whore." Marjorie Majors--a high-class hooker! "Oh really, Marjorie, " I said, an' all that money your mother spent on elocution lessons." By this time the waitress was pourin' the tea into the cream buns! Well, me an' Marjorie--God, we had a great afternoon together. She didn't come lordin' it over me at all. Y'know, she told me about all the places she works-- Bahrain, New York, Munich. An' d' y' know what she told me? When we were at school--she wanted to be like me. The two of us, sittin' there at the *Adelphi,* one's like somethin' out of *Dynasty,* one's like somethin' out the bagwash an' we're havin' a great time confessin' that all those years ago, we each wanted to be the other. I was sad when I thought about it. Like the two of us could have been great mates--y' know, real close. We didn't half get on well together, that afternoon in the *Adelphi.* We were rememberin' all kinds. I could've sat there for ever--neither of us wanted to leave. But then the time caught up with us an' Marjorie had to get her plane. An' y' know somethin'--she didn't want to go. Paris, she had to go to, Paris, France, an' she didn't want to go. An'--an' on the way out--d' y' know what she did? She leaned forward an' just kissed me--there on the cheek--an' there was real affection in that kiss. It was the sweetest kiss I'd known in years. An' then she held my shoulders an' looked at me an' said, "Goodbye, Shirley. Goodbye, Shirley Valentine. (*pause*) On the way home, on the bus, I was cryin'. I don't know why. I'm starin' out the window, tears trippin' down me cheeks. An' in me head there's this voice that keeps sayin', "I used to be Shirley Valentine. I used to be Shirley Valentine... I used to be Shirley..." (*And, indeed, she is now crying.*) What happened? Who turned me into this? I don't want this. Do you remember her, wall? Remember Shirley Valentine? She got married to a boy called Joe an' one day she came to live here. An'--an' even though her name was changed to Bradshaw she was still Shirley Valentine. For a while, She still...knew who she was. She used to ...laugh. A lot. Didn't she? She used to laugh with Joe--when the pair of them did things together, when they made this kitchen together an' painted it together. Remember, wall? Remember when they first painted you an'--an' the silly buggers painted each other as well. Stood here, the pair of them, havin' a paint fight, coverin' each other from head to foot in yellow paint. An' then the two of them, thinkin' they're dead darin', gettin' in the bath--together. And the water was so yellow that he said it was like gettin' a bath in vanilla ice-cream. And Shirley Valentine washed his hair...and kissed his wet head...and knew what happiness meant. What happened, wall? What happened to the pair of them--to Joe, to Shirley Valentine? Did somethin' happen or was it just that nothin' happened? It would be...easier to understand if somethin' had happened, if I'd found him in bed with the

milkman, if--if there was someone to blame. But
there's nothin'. They got married, they made a
home, they had kids and brought them up. And
somewhere along the way the boy called Joe
turned into "him" and Shirley Valentine turned
into this and what I can't remember is the day or
the week or the month or the...when it happened.
When it stopped bein' good. When Shirley
Valentine disappeared, became just another
name on the missin' persons' list. (*She makes a
partially successful attempt to change gear.*) He
says he still loves me, y'know. But he doesn't. It's
just somethin' he says. It's terrible--"I love you"-
-isn't it? Like--like it's supposed to make
everythin' all right. You can be beaten an'
battered an' half-insane an' if you complain he'll
say, he'll say, "What's wrong, y' know I love
you". "I love you." They should bottle it an' sell
it. It cures everythin'. An' d' y' know somethin'?
I've always wondered...why...it is that if
somebody says, "I love you", it seems to
automatically give them the right...to treat you
worse...than people they only like, or people they
don't like at all, or people they couldn't care less
about. See--see, if I wasn't my feller's...wife, if I
was just a next-door neighbour or the man in the
paper shop--he'd talk to me nice. An' he doesn't
say he loves the next-door neighbour or the feller
in the paper shop--he says he loves me! An' he
doesn't talk nice to me. When he talks to me at
all. It's funny, isn't it--"I love you." (*Pause as*

she begins the final stage in the cooking of the meal.) An' I know what you're sayin'. You're sayin' what Jane always says--why don't I leave? An' the fact of the matter is--I don't know why. I don't know why anyone should put up with a situation in which a forty-two year old woman has the opportunity of fulfillin' a dream--of travellin', just a little bit, just two weeks of the year--an' can't do it. I don't know why...I just know that if y' described me to me, I'd say you were tellin' me a joke. I don't know why I stay. I hate it. I hate the joke of it. I hate a life of talkin' to the wall. But I've been talkin' to the wall for more years than I care to remember now. An' I'm frightened. I'm frightened of life beyond the wall. When I was a girl I used to jump off our roof. For fun. Now I get vertigo standin' up in high-heeled shoes. I'm terrified, if y' want to know. I'm terrified that if I left him, I 'd have nowhere to go, an' I'd find that there was no place for me in the life beyond the wall. They'd kept a place reserved for me. For a while. But when it seemed I wan't comin' back they gave the place to someone else-- maybe someone younger, someone who could still talk the language of the place beyond the wall. So I stay. Here. An'--an' if I have to give up goin' to Greece--well...sod it. I mean, after all, what's the Acropolis? It' s only an old-fashioned ruin, isn't it? It's like the DJs say, isn't it? "We're all scousers--there's nothing wrong with us--we've always got a laugh an' a joke haven't we?

They're not like us in London, are they? Not like us in Greece, are they? Greece? Y' know what Greece is, don't y', love? Greece is what y' cook his egg an' chips in." (*She laughs. Pause.*) An' anyway, another bottle of Riesling, I'll be able to pretend this is Greece. Hey, wall...look. (*She goes to the window.*) Look at that sun an' the way it's shinnin'. Look at the sea, the sea. Smell the honeysuckle. Can't y' just taste those olives, those grapes. Look, wall, look at that woman, that lovely woman--doesn't she look serene, sittin' beneath a parasol, at a table by the sea, drinkin' wine in a country where the grape is grown.(*As she lays a plate on the table, the back door opens. Black out*)

Scene 2

The kitchen.   Three weeks later.

A suitcase stands in the kitchen. Shirley enters. She is dressed in a fairly formal and attractive two-piece suit, wears high heels and carries a hat which she places on top of the suitcase, and a large leather handbag/shoulder bag which she places on top of one of the work surfaces. Throughout the scene she constantly double and even triple checks details of the kitchen, contents of cupboards, whereabouts of utensils.

When first she enters she is in a state of nervous agitation.

SHIRLEY. Guess where I'm goin'? Jane's booked a taxi to take us to the airport. She's pickin' me up at four o'clock. (*suddenly*) Four o'clock. (*She checks the clock and her watch.*) Oh jeez, oh jeez. Passport. Passport. (*She checks the contents of her handbag.*) Passport, tickets, money. Passport, tickets, money. Yeh. Oh God, oh God, please say it will be all right. Oh, I feel sick. Those travel pills mustn't be workin'--I still feel sick an' I've taken four already. An' I've only travelled up an' down the stairs. Oh God, passport, tickets, money, passport. I got a full one, a proper passport. Well, you never know, Shirley--it could be the start of somethin'--this year Greece, next year...the world. (*She slaps the passport shut with a cry of strained anguish.*) Oh, I know I should have told him. I know it would have been easier if I'd told him. It wouldn't though, would it, wall? If I'd told him he would have talked me out of it. He would have found a way. He would have made me feel guilty. Guilty? As if I don't feel guilty enough as it is. Three weeks, secretly gettin' all me things ready. It's been like livin' in bleedin' Colditz with a tunnel beneath the floorboards an' every soddin' sound y' think it's the SS, comin' for y'--they've found out about the tunnel. (*She looks up.*) God. God, I know...I'm bein' cruel. I know I'll

have to pay for it, when I get back. But I don't
mind payin' for it then. Just...just do me a big
favour, God, an' don't make me have to pay for it
durin' this fortnight. Don't let anythin' happen
to our Millandra, our Brian. An' keep Joe safe.
Please. (*pause*) Three weeks secretly ironin' an'
packin' an' cookin' all his meals for this two
weeks. They're all in the freezer. Me mother's
gonna come in an' defrost them an' do his
cookin'. With a bit of luck "he" won't even
notice I'm not here. Oh, you should've told him.
Y' should have, Shirley. Shirley, y' silly bitch.
How could you have told him an' still been able to
go? I know, I know. An' look what happened over
his chips an' egg. I know, I know. (*pause*) Keep
thinkin' about the chips an' egg, keep thinkin'
about the...It was that that decided me, wasn't it,
wall? I'd cooked those chips lovely, hadn't I? In
oil. An' they were free range those eggs. I mean,
all right, so he was expectin' steak but...he sits
down at that table, doesn't he, an' he looks at this
plate of egg an' chips. Just looks. Doesn't make
any effort to pick up his knife an' fork. He sits
there, with this dead quizzical look on his face,
an' he's starin' at the plate, studyin' it, y' know
as though it contains the meanin' of life. Well, I
just ignored him, didn't I? I just sat there, at the
other end of the table. Well, eventually, he goes,
"What's this? What. Is. This?" I said to him, I
said, "Well, when I cooked it, it was egg an'
chips, an' as neither of us is a magician I'

assuming it still is egg an' chips." Well, he
leaned back in his chair an' he said "I am
not...eating shite", honest to God, an' he pushed
the plate the entire length of the table. Well, I'm
sittin there, then, aren't I? With a lap full of egg
an' chips. I've got yolk drippin' down me leg an'
"he" has started talkin' to the fridge. "Cos he
does that, when he' narked, doesn't he, wall? If
he's in a real nark he always talks to the cooker
or the fridge or the mantelpiece. "I'm pullin' me
tripe out from mornin' till night", he's tellin' the
fridge, "an' what does she give me when I get
home". Well, of course, the fridge never answers
him so whenever he asks it a question, he always
answers it himself. He always goes--"I'll tell y'
what she gives me. Chips an' egg, chips an'
fuckin' egg she gives me." Well, I don't know
what possessed me but while he was screamin' at
the fridge, I picked meself up from the table,
cleaned meself down as best I could, got hold of a
pen an' wrote, across the wall, in big letters--
GREECE. He didn't even notice, 'cos by this time
he's givin' the cooker an' the fridge his
impression of Arthur Scargill deliverin' the
Gettysburg Address. Well, I just walked out. I got
me coat an' went round to our Millandra's flat.
But there was no-one in. I just walked round the
block a few times. I was gonna phone Jane, but
all the phones were out of order. They always are,
aren't they? Well, they are round here--even the
vandals are complainin'. I must have walked

round for about an hour. I wanted to go an' see
someone, someone I could talk to. But there
wasn't anyone. I never felt so alone in me
whole life. I used to know so many people. Where
does everyone go to? In the end I just came back
here. He'd been to a Chinese take-away.
"What's that?" he said to me, pointin' at the
wall. "It's a place," I said. "It's a place I'm goin
to." "I'm not goin' to no Greece," he said. "If
that's why I'm not gettin' fed properly, because
you're savin' up for a foreign holiday, y' can
forget it." Well, that's when I started laughin'. I
ended up--I was hysterical--I ended up rollin' on
the kitchen floor. He just stepped over me,
walked out. But I couldn't stop laughin' because I
knew then. I knew I was gonna do it. I knew I
was gonna got to Greece. An' everythin' went
marvellous, didn't it? I made all the
arrangements, got a passport. I was quite
impressed with meself. So yesterday I thought I'd
nip into town an' get a few last-minute things,
know the way y' do? Well, as I passed Marks and
Spencer's I looked in the window an' y' know
they had some lovely underwear on display, y'
know dead silky. A little bit Janet Reger but only
half the price. Well, normally I'm a bit
conservative--next to the skin as it were--but I
thought, oh, go on, give y'self a treat, it's the sort
of stuff that'd be nice and cool in a hot climate. So
I get into Marks, I bought a new bra, a couple of
slips, a few pairs of pants an' I 'm standin' there

waitin' for them to be wrapped. Well, who comes
up to me but "her" from next door. Gillian. Well,
what's she like, wall? What's Gillian like? I'm
not sayin' she's a bragger, but if you've been to
Paradise, she's got a season ticket. Y'know she's
that type--if you've got a headache, she's got a
brain tumour. "Oh, hello, Shirley," she says,
'cos that's how she talks, know she begrudes y'
the breath. "Hello, Shirley, oh they're nice," she
said, spottin' me little garments. "It's
marvellous what they can do with man-made
fibres these days, isn't it?" An' she's pickin' up
one of me slips y' know, havin' a really good
gawp at it. "You'd almost think it was silk. If
you weren't familiar with the real thing." I said
to meself, "Keep your mouth shut, Shirley."
Because y' can't win with her. Well, she dropped
the slip back on the counter an' then she said,
"But I suppose they will look quite nice on your
Millandra". Well, I know I should've kept me
mouth shut but that got me really riled an' I
suddenly heard meself sayin', "Oh no, Gillian,
these aren't for Millandra, I'm buyin' these for
meself. Of course, I shan't be wearin' them for
meself, I shall be wearin' them for my lover."
Well, her jaw dropped into her handbag. For
once she couldn't top it an' I got a bit carried
away then, I heard meself sayin', "Yes, Gillian,
we fly out tomorrow, my lover and I, for a
fortnight in the Greek Islands--just two weeks of
sun, sand, taramasalata an' whatever else takes

our fancy. Well, I must be goin', Gillian--I've
still got a few things to buy. I don't suspose you've
noticed which counter the garter belts are on? Oh,
well, never mind, I'll find them. Ta-ra,
Gillian", and' I was off before she could get her
wits together an' tell me about the two-year fling
she's been havin' with Robert Redford. "Course,
all the way home on the bus I'm thinkin' "Oh,
you silly bitch, why did you say that? What
happens if she calls round tonight--while "he" is
in? What happens if she just lets it slip?" "Cos
she's like that, Gillian, y'know she's got more
news than Rupert Murdock. But when I got home
I forgot all about Gillian. When I got home, what
was waitin' for me? Our Millandra, with all her
bags an' cases. "I hate that Sharron-Louise," she
said. "She's a mare. Mother, I've come back to
live with you." Well, I'm stood here lookin' at
her, me jaw's dropped half-way to Australia.
"Mother," she says, "Will y' make me some
Horlicks an' toast--like y' used to?" Then she
was off. Up the stairs to her old room. Well, I
made the toast an' the Horlicks--took it up to her.
She's got herself into bed, sittin' there propped up
with two pillows, readin' her old *Beano* annuals.
"I love you, Mother," she said, "I don't know why
I went to live with that cow in the first place--
Mother, y' haven't put enough sugar in the
Horlicks, will y' get us another spoon?" Well, I
go down, get the sugar, bring it back, stir it up for
her an' she's sayin' "We'll go down town on

Saturday, shall we, Mother? We'll do a bit of shoppin', eh Mother, just you an' me". An' the thing is, I was noddin'. She hadn't been back ten minutes an' I' d gone straight into bein' "Auto-Mother". She's got me struttin' round like R2 bleedin' D2. Well, it was when she asked me to bring the t.v. upstairs for her that me head cleared. Instead of goin' downstairs again I sat on the edge of the bed an' I said, "Millandra, I'm really pleased you've come back home because I've missed y'. I mean, I've never said that or whinged an' whined because, because I believe that kids have to have their own lives. But there's many a time y' know, many a time that I would have loved to sit down with y' an' talk, go to town with y', have a meal with y', share a laugh, just, like not as your mother but as another human bein'. But I couldn't because you had your own life, your own friends, your own interests--none of it to do with me." "Well, we'll be able to do all that now, " she said, "because I've come back home." "And that's fantastic," I said. "An' you couldn't have picked a better time--it'll be a great help havin' you here to look after your father." Well, this look came on her face. "What's wrong with him?" she said. "Oh, there's nothin wrong with him," I assured her, "but y' know with me not bein' here, with me an' Jane goin' to Greece tomorrow." Well, d' y' know, it was like her hot water bottle had sprung a leak. "What?" she yelled, "Yeh", I said, "I'm going to Greece for a

fortnight." "You," she said, "you going' to
Greece, what for?" "For two weeks," I said. Well
she flounces out of the bed. "That Jane one, an'
you," she's goin', "in Greece. An' what's me
father had to say about that?" Well, when I said I
hadn't told him, she went mental. She started
gettin' dressed, "I think it's a disgrace," she's
goin', "two middle-aged women goin' on their
own to Greece--I think it's disgustin'." An' she's
straight down the stairs an' on the phone, tellin'
Sharron-Louise that she's comin' back to the flat.
Well, I'm sittin' there upstairs an' then it
suddenly struck me--her sayin' I was
disgustin'. I mean she 's jumpin' to the same
conclusions as her father would. She thinks I'
must goin' off on a grab-a-granny fortnight.
Well, I started to get narked. The more I thought
about it, the more riled I got. I was gonna go down
an' give her a piece of me mind but I heard the
front door slam. I went to the window an' she's
loadin' her things into a taxi. Well, I flung the
window open an' I shouted, "Yes, that's right,
Millandra--I'm goin' to Greece for the sex; sex
for breakfast, sex for dinner, sex for tea an' sex
for supper." Well, she just ignored me but this
little cab driver leans out an' pipes up, "That
sounds like a marvellous diet, love." "It is," I
shouted back, "have y' never heard of it? It's
called the 'F' Plan." Well, our Millandra
slammed the taxi door an' off they went down the
street. I just sat there in our Millandra's

bedroom. I was livid at first but when I calmed down I just felt...felt like a real fool. All I could think about was Millandra sayin', "What for? You goin' to Greece--what for?" Kids--they can't half destroy your confidence, can't they? I'd spent three weeks tellin' meself I could do it, that I'd be all right, be able to go, be able to enjoy meself. I'd even convinced meself that I wan't really that old, that me hips weren't really as big as I thought they were, that me belly was quite flat for a woman who'd had two kids. That me stretch marks wouldn't really be noticeable to anyone but me. I'd even let that sales girl at C&A sell me a bikini. But sittin' there on our Millandra's bed, after she'd said that---I suddenly had thighs that were thicker than the pillars in the Parthenon. Me stretch marks were as big as tyre marks on the M6 an' instead of goin' to Greece I should be applyin' for membership of the pensioners' club. I'm sittin' there thinkin', maybe our Millandra's right. "You goin' to Greece. What for?" Maybe she's right, maybe it is pathetic. What am I goin' for? I mean, it might be easier not to go, to stay here. Where I'm safe. Where's there's no risk. For three weeks I'd been buildin' up this marvellous picture of what it would be like, how I was goin' to feel with the sun on me an' the ocean everywhere. But after she'd said that I couldn't...couldn't get the picture back, into me mind. I couldn't bring back the feelin' I'd had. I just sat there thinkin',

"Shirley you are one silly bitch. Just another stupid woman who thinks she can have an adventure, when the time for adventures is over." "What for?", I kept askin' meself. I thought about the bikini I'd bought an' I felt ashamed. I felt embarrassed at me own stupidity, at lettin' meself think it was possible. "What for?" "What am I goin' for?" An' of course the truth of the matter was that I was goin' for the excitement of not knowing; not knowing where I was goin', not knowing what would happen, not knowing what the place would be like or look like, not knowin' the foreign language I'd hear, not knowin', for the first time since before I could remember, exactly what the days would hold for me. It was the excitement of somethin' that was foreign, to me. The excitement of jumpin' off our roof. An' when our Millandra had said that, it was like she'd caught me, on the roof, just as I was about to jump an' she'd said, "Ey, you'll break your bloody neck. Get down off there an' don't be so stupid". An' I hesitated, an' in that moment I saw how big the drop was, an' how hard the ground was an' how fragile me bones were. An' I realized that I was too old for jumpin' off the roof. I went downstairs, to phone Jane, to phone me mother an' tell her she needn't bother comin' in for the fortnight. I'd even picked up the phone. But the doorbell went an' I put the phone down an' went to the door. Gillian was stood there. "Oh, hello Shirley, " she said, "is Joe at home?" Well, I just laughed. "No, Joe's not in, Gillian. But listen, if you've come to spill the beans y' might as well..." But she just pushed past me, came into the house. "I don't want to spill any beans, Shirley," she said, "I just wanted to check that Joe wasn't in before I gave you this." An' she handed me this beautifully wrapped package. "I want you to have this, Shirley. It's never been worn. You see, " she said, "I was never...brave enough. Oh, Shirley," she said, "how I wish I had. How I wish I'd had your...bravery."   With that she went to the door. Just as she was goin' out she said to me--"You're brave, Shirley. I just want you to know, I think you're marvellous." An' she was gone. I opened up the package. (*She opens her suitcase.*) It was this. (*She produces a superb silk robe.*) Silk. Gillian was right--there's nothin' like the real thing. It must have been bought years an' years ago. It's got the original label--The Bon Marche. I didn't even dare try it on at first. I felt awful, about what I'd said to Gillian, about taking a lover. I mean, I didn't think she'd really believe me. But she had. Completely believed me. Gillian believed that it was perfectly possible for me to be some marvellous, brave, living woman. I got me mirror out an' looked at meself, an' tried to see the woman that Gillian had seen in me. In Gillian's eyes I was no longer Shirley the neighbour, Shirley the middle-aged mother, Shirley Bradshaw. I had become Shirley the

Sensational, Shirley the Brave, Shirley Valentine. An' even if I couldn't see it in the mirror, even if none of it was true about me takin' a lover an' all that rubbish--the point is that Gillian had believed it. Believed it was possible of me. I tried the robe on. It was perfect. It was beautiful. An' in that moment...so was I. In that moment our roof wouldn't have been high enough for me. I could have jumped off a skyscraper. An' now the day's here. An' I'm goin' to the land beyond the wall. I'm gonna sit an' eat olives on a Greek seafront. An' I don't even like olives. But I might like them in Greece. They eat squid y' know. An' octopus-- they do. An' I'm gonna eat it too. I don't care. I'm gonna do everythin'. I'm gonna try anything. Like I used to. Unafraid. Without fear of anythin' new. I'll be Shirley the Brave. "Course, I'm terrified really. But I'm not gonna let it stop me from enjoyin' things. I don't mean I'm gonna be a girl again--because you can never be that; but instead of sayin' "Christ, I'm forty-two". I'm gonna say--"Shirley, you're only forty-two, isn't that marvellous". (*She looks at herself in the mirror.*) Not bad, not bad. Oh, hold on, hold on. (*She places the hat on her head and examines the effect in the mirror.*) What do you think, wall? Oh, shut up, wall, I'm not talkin' to you anymore. *(She smiles at herself in the mirror.)* Well, that's it, Shirley--all dolled up an' ready to go. Case packed? Case packed.

Passport, tickets, money? Passport, tickets, money. (*She closes her handbag and sits with it, on the suitcase. She takes a last glance at the kitchen to see if everything has been left in order. It has.*) Four o'clock Jane's pickin' me up. (*She looks at her watch.*) Twenty past two. (*Black-out*)

ACT II

A Greek island

A secluded section of shore, dotted with rocks and baked by the Mediterranean sun. It is an underdeveloped corner of the bay, a place not yet appropriated by tourists. In the background we see a hint of the village and the taverna. The deep blue of the sky dominates. A white table with some chairs has been placed in this spot.

> *When the Curtain rises, the parasol is still folded. There is a piece of rush-matting laid out for sunbathing.*

SHIRLEY *enters. She has bare feet and wears Gillian's robe over cut-down denims and a bikini top.*

SHIRLEY. I'll bet y' didn't recognize me, did y'? I hardly recognize meself these days. D' y' like me tan? (*She opens the robe to display a deep tan.*) It's marvellous, isn't it? I love it here--don't I, rock? (*She points to the rock.*) That's rock. We met the first day I got here, didn't we? Well, I

46

didn't want to go down on to the beach, y' see. I
thought I'd get a bit of a tan before I ventured on to
the beach because--let's face it--I was so white. If
I'd walked on to that beach when I first got here,
they would have thought I'd just had a fresh coat of
while emulsion. When I first arrived there was
more glare comin' off me than there was off the
sun. So what I did was I found this little place--I
found you, didn't I, rock? I talked to you. Rock.
He's got his name written all the way through
him. 'Course, I talk to rock--but he doesn't talk
back to me. Well he can't, can he? It's a Greek
rock. It doesn't understand a bleedin' word I'm
sayin'. I might have risked the beach if I'd been
with Jane. But on me own I felt a bit--y'know,
conspicuous. Jane met a feller, didn't she? Not
here, on the plane--honest to God. An' the state of
him. I wouldn't give y' tuppence a ton. Sporty
type--y' know, all groin an' Adidas labels.
Ooogh. Designer teeth he had. An' bloodshot eyes.
Y' know when he smiled with these blazin' white
teeth an' the bloodshot eyes, I said to Jane,"Oh, he
must be a Liverpool supporter". She didn't like
that. But I didn't care. I'd got past carin' to tell y'
the truth. I mean, we were gonna do everythin'
together. We hadn't even landed an' she's got
herself fixed up. She only went to the loo. When
she got back she said to me, "Erm, I've just been
invited out to dinner. Tonight." Well, I looked at
her. "Pardon," I said. "Yeh," she said, "I've just
met this chap, sittin' up at the back. He's stayin'

at a villa on the other side of the island an' he's
invited me over for dinner. Tonight. Oh Shirley,
you don't mind, do you?" Well I didn't say
anythin'. There was nothin' I could say, was
there? I just stared out the window of the plane an'
I thought, "D' y' know, if I had a parachute, I'd get
off now." I even considered gettin' off without a
parachute actually. 'Course, she was sayin' to
me--"It's only for tonight. We'll still do all the
things we planned, Shirley." But I knew. Me
instinct told me I'd hardly see her again after
that. An' I didn't want her to be spendin' time
with me when she'd rather be elsewhere. I didn't
want her pityin' me. "Listen, Jane, "I said, "I
think you've probably blown the feminist of the
year award--so will y' just leave it out, right?
Obviously," I said, "it's been a difficult time for
you since your feller ran off with the milkman
and now that you've got this opportunity I don't
want y' to give even a thought to me. You just go
off to his villa an' enjoy yourself an' give his
olives a good pressing." D'y' know what she said
to me? "Thanks for being' so understandin'."
An' she never came back that night, y' know. Or
the next mornin'. She never came back for the
first four days. They must've been marvellous
olives. I was just left on me own. I was alone. But
I wasn't lonely. Well, I'm an expert at it really.
But what I found was--if you're a woman, alone, it
doesn't half seem to upset people; like whenever I
walked into the dinin'-room at the hotel it was

like everyone was lookin' at me. I've got this little table to meself, an' it's lovely. I just love sittin' there, in the evenin'. But on the third day, I'm sat there, at me table. I've been sunbathin' all day. I'm glowin' like a lobster an' feelin' dead content an' quiet. I was in such a trance, I hadn't even noticed this woman come across. She was talkin' to me before I realized she was there. "We couldn't help notice you were alone, dear," she says to me. "Would y' like to come an' join us at our table? There is a spare place." Well, I was shattered. I didn't want to join anyone. I didn't wanna talk. I wanted to be quiet. But she's standin' there, waitin' for me to say somethin'. An' then I notice that the whole of the restaurant's waitin' to see what would happen to the woman on her own. Well, of course, I coundn't say no, could I? I mean, the woman was only bein' kind, wasn't she? But inside I was cursin'. Well, d' y'know, as I sat down at their table, with her an' her husband, it was like the whole restaurant let out this great sigh of relief, as if me bein' on me own had been like a great problem for everyone, an' now it had been solved, everyone could relax, everyone could talk louder an' laugh; I thought the waiters were gonna break into applause 'cos I'd been rescued from me loneliness by Jeanette an' Dougie. Jeanette an' Dougie Walsh--from Manchester. Well, I know the exact dimensions of her kitchen, the price of the new extension, the colour of the microwave an' the contents of the Hoover, an' we

hadn't even started on the first course; it's a good
job it wasn't soup--I would've put me head in it an'
drowned meself. It wasn't until we got to the main
course that they even acknowledged we were in
Greece. An' then I wish they hadn't bothered.
Everythin' was wrong--the sun was too hot for
them, the sea was too wet for them, Greece too
Greek for them. They were that type, y'know, if
they'd been at the Last Supper they would have
asked for chips. An' I wouldn't mind but the
family on the next table joined in as well an'
started complainin' about everythin'. An' I'm
sittin' there dead embarrassed out of me mind
because there's this poor Greek waiter tryin' to
serve our main course an' he's got to listen to this
lot goin' on about his country as though it's in the
Fourth World. This feller on the table next to us is
sayin' to Dougie, "'Ave y' not seent bloody fishin'
boats out theer int bay? 'Ave y' not seen 'em, 'ave
y' not? Bloody hell, what they like, love?" he says
to his wife, "What did I say to you when I saw
them boats int bay. I said to her, I did, I said them
boats, if y' look at side of 'em ant find name of t'
boatbuilder, I'll bet y' a pound to a penny it says
Noah. Din't I? I bloody did. Ay." An' they're all
roarin' with laughter. Well, I was so ashamed I
couldn't keep me mouth shut any longer. "Excuse
me," I said to the feller on the next table, "excuse
me. You do watch the Olympic Games I take it?
An' y' do know, I suppose, that it was the Greeks
who invented the Olympic Games?" Well, they

were all lookin' at me. "Oh yes," I said, "the Greeks were responsible for many things. In fact it was the Greeks who were responsible for the most important invention of all--the wheel." 'Course I didn't know if it had been invented by the Greeks, the Irish or the cavemen but I didn't care. Once I'd opened me mouth there was no stoppin' me. "The English," I'm goin', "the English? Don't talk to me about the English, because whilst the Greeks were buildin' roads an' cities an' temples, what were the English doin'? I'll tell y' what the English were doin', they were runnin' round in loin cloths an' ploughin' up the earth with the arse-bone of a giraffe." Well, I hadn't meant to get so carried away. I suddenly realized how loud I'd been shoutin'. Everyone's lookin' at me--the feller an' his family on the next table have turned away an' Dougie an' Jeanette are sittin' there wonderin' why they asked this lunatic to join them. Well, Dougie obviously decides to use diversionary tactics an' he says to the waiter who's just walkin' away, "Hey, mate. What is this?" An' he points to his plate. The waiter says to him, "Eet ees calamares, sir." "Yeh, but what I'm askin' y'," Dougie says, "what I'm askin' y', is what is it? "Erm...eet's calamares, sir, eet's a type of er...feesh." Well, Dougie looks at his plate an' he's not convinced. "It don't look much like fish to me," he says. "My wife's got a very delicate stomach. She's very particular about what she eats. Are you sure this is

fish?" "Sir, I can...promees you," says the waiter,
"eet ees feesh. Eet ees feesh...was pulled from the
sea thees morning, by my own father. In a boat
called *Noah*." Well, the silence at our table is
deafenin'. We're all sittin' there eatin' an' no-
one's sayin' a word. I'm feeling like a right heel
because I've upset them all an' I'm tryin' to think
of somethin' to say that'll make it all right. Well
y'know what it's like when--when there's one of
those silences an' you've got to force yourself to
find somethin' to say--you always come out with
the wrong thing, don't y'? Well, what I said was,
"The squid's very nice, isn't it?" The pair of them
stopped eatin' an' looked at me. "Pardon me?"
Jeanette said. "The squid," I said, pointin' to her
plate, "the squid, the octopus, it's quite nice really,
isn't...?" Well, it was funny the way Jeanette
fainted. Y' know, sort of in slow motion. As she
comes round I'm tryin' to apologize an'
everythin', but they were off--out--away. They
didn't eat in the hotel after that. Apparently they
found this restaurant at the back of the hotel that
does proper Greek food--doner kebabs. After
dinner, whilst everyone else was makin' their
way to the bar, I went up to me room an' grabbed
me light coat an' I walked out of the hotel an' into
this lovely night outside. *(pause, as she
remembers it)* Well that's when I met him.
Y'know--Christopher Columbus. That's not his
real name. His real name's Costas. But I call
him Christopher. Christopher Columbus. I'll bet

y' don't know why I call him that? It's because
he's got a boat. Well, it's his brother's boat
actually. An because it's er--he, we--discovered
it. The island of clitoris. I'm terrible, aren't I? I
suppose y' think I'm scandalous--a married
woman, forty-two, got grown-up kids. I suppose y'
think I'm wicked. Jane does. "Shirley," she said,
"you're acting like a stupid teenager. I suppose
the next think you're going to tell me is that the
earth trembled." "Trembled?" I said. "Jane, I
thought there's been an earthquake. It was at least
point nine on the Richter Scale." "Oh spare me the
details," she's goin', "spare me the details."
Well she wasn't half jealous. But y' see, it wasn't
my fault; if she hadn't gone off, with the walkin'
groin, in the first place--I never would have met
Christopher Columbus. (*pause*) He kissed me
stretch marks, y' know. He did. He said--he said
they were lovely...because they were a part of
me...an' I was lovely. He said--he said, stretch
marks weren't to be hidden away; they were to be
displayed, to be proud of. He said my stretch
marks showed that I was alive, that I'd
survived...that they were marks of life. (*pause*)
Aren't men full of shit? I mean, can you imagine
him, the mornin' after he's given me this speech--
he wakes up an' he finds *his* belly has got all these
lines runnin' across it? I mean, can y' see him?
Rushin' to the mirror an' goin', "Fantastic.
Fuckin' fantastic. I've got stretch marks. At
last!" But the thing about him, the thing about

Costas was, when he gave y' a load of guff--*he* believed it. What was marvellous about him was he never made y' feel at all threatened. An' he understood how to talk with a woman. That's the first thing I noticed about him. "Cos, y' know, most men, really, they're no good at talkin' with women. They don't know how to listen or they feel that they have to take over the conversation. Like...with most fellers, if you said somethin' like--like, "My favourite season is autumn." Well, most feller's go, "Is it? My favourite season's spring. See, what I like about spring is that in spring..." Then y' get ten minutes of why he likes spring. An' you weren't talkin about spring--you were talkin' about autumn. So what d' y' do. You end up talkin' about what he wants to talk about. Or you don't talk at all. Or you wind up talkin' to y'self. An' whichever way it works out it always ends up that there's no talkin' goin' on. It just becomes words. Words without meanin'. Words that get spoken...but die...because they have nowhere to go. But it wasn't like that with Costas. When I came out the hotel that night I just walked down the little esplanade. There was hardly a soul about, but I noticed the light was on in the taverna an' outside the front of it there's these tables, with white parasols. Well I'm sittin' there an' he came out to serve me. "Erm, excuse me," I said to him, "I know this sounds a bit soft but would you mind...I mean would you object if I moved this table an'

chair over there, by the edge of the sea?" Well, he
looked at me for a minute. "You want," he said,
"you want move table and chair to the sea? What
for? You don't like here at my bar?" "Oh yeh," I
said, "yeh, it's a lovely bar but--but I've just got
this soft little dream about sittin' at a table by the
sea." "Ah," he said, an' he smiled. "A dream, a
dream. We move this table to the edge of the sea, it
make your dream come true?" "Erm, yeh," I
said. "I think so." "Then, is no problem. I move
the table for you. And tonight when I serve in my
bar, I say to customer--'tonight, tonight I make
someone's dream come true'." Well, I thought for
a second he was bein' sarcastic--'cos in England
it would have been. But no, he carries the table an'
chair over here an' he brings me out this glass of
wine I've ordered. Well, I paid him an' thanked
him but he said to me, "No, I thank you. Enjoy
your dream", then he gave a little bow an' he was
gone, back to the taverna, leavin' me alone with
the sea an' the sky an' me soft little dream..
Well, it's funny, isn't it, but y'know if you've
pictured somethin', y' know, if you've imagined
how somethin's gonna be, made a picture of it in
your mind, well it never works out, does it? I
mean for weeks I'd had this picture of meself,
sittin' here, sittin' here, drinkin' wine by the sea;
I even knew exactly how I was gonna feel. But
when it got to it, it wasn't a bit like that. Because
when it got to it, I didn't feel at all lovely an'
serene. I felt pretty daft actually. A bit stupid an'--

an' awfully, awfully old. What I kept thinkin'
about was how I'd lived such a little life. An' one
way or another even that would be over pretty
soon. I thought to meself, my life has been a crime
really--against God, because...I didn't live it
fully. I'd allowed myself to live this little life
when inside me there was so much. So much more
that I could have lived a bigger life with--but it had
all gone unused, an' now it never would be. Why-
-why do y'get...all this life, when it can't be used?
Why--do y' get...all these...feelin's an' dreams
an' hopes if they can't ever be used. That's where
Shirley Valentine disappeared to. She got lost in
all this unused life. An' that's what I was
thinkin', sittin' there on me own, starin' out at the
sea, me eyes open wide an' big tears splashin'
down from them. I must've sat there for ages
because the noise from the hotel bar had died away
an' even the feller from the taverna was lockin'
up for the night. He came to collect me glass. It
was still full. I hadn't even taken a sip. He saw
that I was cryin' but he didn't say anythin'. He
just sat down, on the sand an' stared out at the sea.
An' when I'd got over it, when it was all right to
talk, he said, "Dreams are never in the places we
expect them to be." I just smiled at him. "Come, "
he said, "I escort you back to your hotel." An' he
did. An' he told me his name was Costas an' I told
him my name was Shirley. An' when we got to the
front door of the hotel he said to me, "Tomorrow,
you want, to come with me? I take my brother's

boat. We go all round the island?" I just shook me
head, "No, I said, "it's all right. You've been dead
kind as it is. Thank you." "Is no problem, I come
for you, early." "No," I'm goin', "thanks but..."
"You afraid?" he suddenly said. "No," I said,
"but..." "You afraid," he said, nodding, "you
afraid I make try to foak with you." I didn't know
where to put meself, but he just laughed. "Of
course I like to foak with you. You are lovely
woman. Any man be crazy not to want to foak
with you. But I don't ask to foak. I ask you want to
come my brother's boat--is different thing. Foak
is foak, boat is boat. I come fetch you tomorrow. I
bring wine, I bring food and we go. Tomorrow, I
just make you happy. No need to be sad, no need to
be afraid. I give my word of honour I don't try to
make foak with you." Well, what could I say?
"Well, I'll--erm--I'll see y' in the morning'
then." "Course, the next mornin' I've just got
dressed. I'm sittin in me room, there's this
knockin' on me door, I thought, "Oh Christ, he's
come up to me room." Well, I opened the door, an'
guess what? Jane's back! "Shirley, I know I've
been awful but please, please forgive me. I'll
make it up to you. Come on, it's still early, let's go
and hire a car and drive out round the island."
Well, what could I do? I mean she had paid for me
to be there. If it hadn't been for Jane I never would
have been in Greece in the first place. She keeps
askin' me if I forgive her. "Of course I forgive
y'," I said, an' she threw her arms round me then.

"Come on," she said, "let's put it all behind us
now. Let's make today the real start of our
holiday. I know you've had an awful time and
Shirley I'm sorry. Have you just been sitting here
in your room the past few days? I know you.
Without me being here I suppose you've just been
sitting here talking to the wall, haven't you?"
"Well, " I thought to meself, "how does she see
me? Does she think I'm an old-aged pensioner or
a five-year old child?" "I'll only be a few
minutes," she's sayin', "I'll just pick up a few
things from my room." Well, it was just as she
got to the door that there was a knock on it. She
pulled it open an' Costas was there. She took one
look at him an' said, "What is it, room service?
Did you order anything, Shirley?" But Costas just
walked straight past her an' into the room.
"Shirley, Shirley, you come, you come. You late. I
wait for you on the quay. I already put the wine,
the food on the boat. I stand, I wait an' then I think,
'Ah, Shirley and me, we get to bed so late last
night, Shirley she must have oversleep." "Well,
the look on Jane's face could've turned the milk."
"Quickly now you get ready. Don't need bring
much clothing. I wait on quay for you. Hurry."
An' as he passes Jane he goes, "Apology for
interrupting you. Now you continue cleaning the
room." Well, if Jane had kept her mouth shut, if
she hadn't tried to treat me like a child, I might
have run after Costas an' said I couldn't go, or
could me friend come as well. But she said,

"Shirley. What do you think you're playing at?" I
didn't say a word. I just looked at her. She was
goin' on about how I'd never been abroad before.
When she got to the bit about, "men like that, these
Greek islanders who are just waiting for bored,
middle-aged women to fall into their..."I just
stormed straight past her an' out. I steered the
boat, y'know. See me on that bridge--natural. I
mean, I knew I wasn't the first woman on that
boat an' I certainly wouldn't be the last. But I
knew I was with a good man. I knew that
whatever happened he wouldn't take anythin'
from me. We sailed for miles an' miles. An' we
talked. Properly. An' we didn't half laugh. We
liked each other. An' isn't it funny, but if you're
with someone who likes y', who sort of, approves of
y', well y' like--like start to grow again. Y' move
in the right way, say the right thing at the right
time. An' you're not eighteen or forty-two or
sixty-four. You're just alive. An' I know if I could
have seen myself that day I would have said,
"Look at that lovely woman, riding on the sea.
Look at that lovely woman, swimming." Well, I
know I'd left me swimmin' costume in the hotel.
So what? We'd parked the boat an' was lookin'
over the side. I said, "How deep do you think it is
here, Costas?" "Mm. Maybe a thousand metres--
maybe ten thousand metres, who knows. Maybe so
deep it goes on forever." An' when I stood there, on
the edge of the boat, naked as the day I was born,
about to jump into this water that was as deep as

forever, I felt as strong an' as excited an' as
bloody mad as I did when I jumped off our roof.
The two of us just splashed an' laughed an' swam
in the water an' I knew Costas would keep his
promise but I didn't want him to because it was the
most natural thing in the world. So I swan up to
him. An' I put me arms around him an' kissed
him. An' that's when I nicknamed him
Christopher Columbus. Mind you, I could just as
easily have named him Andre Previn--I don't
know where this orchestra came from. Later on,
just lyin' there on the boat, with the sun beginnin'
to dip towards the evenin', that's when the thought
came to me. I tried to like, push it out of me head at
first. Because it was too shocking. I kept tryin' to
think of other things, to make this thought go
away. But it wouldn't. It was just there in me
head. An' this thought was: "If... somehow... if...
for...some...reason...I...didn't...go...back...
home... who would really care? Would it cause
anyone real suffering? Would it damage
anyone? Who would miss--me? Why should I go
back? Why should I go back an' become that
woman again when--when that woman isn't
needed anymore. Her job's done. She's brought up
her kids." I mean, they'd say it was awful, it was
terrible to have a mother who went on holiday an'
never came back. I hadn't gone round the pipe. I
hadn't. I hadn't fallen in love with Costas. It had
been sweet. It had been lovely. It had been a day
full of kindness. But I hadn't fallen in love with

him. I'd fallen in love with the idea of livin'. An'
every day, when I woke up, when I came down
here with Jane, when we went an ' had a coffee or
a drink at Costas's taverna, when I was lyin' in
me bed, just droppin' off to sleep, it was always
there in me head--this shocking thought--"I'm not
goin' back. I'm not goin' back." *(pause)* An', of
course, all the time I knew really. I knew I'd have
to go back in the end. I knew that I was just one of
millions before me who'd gone on a holiday an'
had such a good time that they didn't want to go
home. Because we don't do what we want to do. We
do what we have to do. An' pretend it's what we
want to do. An' what I wanted to do was to stay
here and be Shirley Valentine. An' what I had to
do was to go back there, back to being' St. Joan of
the Fitted Units. An' all through the days, an'
when I said goodbye to Costas, an' on the way to the
airport, an' in the long queue for the check-in
desk, I didn't know if I'd do what I wanted to do, or
what I had to do. We were standin' there, in this
queue, me an' Jane an' all the others who had to go
back. An' I remembered this question I was
gonna ask Jane. So I said to her, "Jane, Jane, why
is it that there's all this unused life?" She just said
it was because of men, it was all the fault of men,
an' went back to readin' her magazine. An' I
thought about it, an' I thought: "That's
rubbish...it's not just men who do it to women.
Because I've looked at Joe, an' I know it's the
same for him. He had more life in him than he

could use. An' so he carries all this...waste
around with him. It's the same for everyone. I
know it. When I'm out, when I'm in the shops,
when I see people I grew up with, standin' there in
the shop buyin' vegetables. An' we say how are y',
we all say fine, an' we pretend we are because the
vegetables are fresh an' we haven't had a cold this
year an' our kids grew up with their limbs intact
an' never got into trouble with the police. We say
we're fine. An' we carry on an' on an' on until
we die. An' most of us die...long before we're
dead. An' what kills us is the terrible weight of all
this unused life that we carry round." We'd got to
the check-in desk. Me suitcase was on the
conveyor belt with a tag on it for England, for
home. I stood there, just watchin' it as it moved
away, along the conveyor belt an' through those
flaps an' disappeared into this dark hole. An' I
knew then. I knew I couldn't go with it...Jane just
called out at first, as she saw me walkin' away.
Then she realized, she knew an' she screamed at
me to come back, to come back. All the people in
the queue were lookin' at me. An' I knew they all
wanted me to "come back, come back". But I just
kept walkin', across the concourse. All I had left
was me handbag, the clothes I stood up in,
Gillian's robe, me passport an' a few drachmas.
An' after I'd paid me bus fare, even the drachmas
had gone. (*pause*) When I walked up to the
taverna, Costas was talkin' to this woman, sittin'
on a bar stool. As I walked in I heard him sayin'

to her: "You afraid? You afraid I want make try
to". The poor feller, he nearly dropped his olives
when he saw me. "Don't worry, Costas," I said, "I
haven't come back for you. I've come back for the
job. The job in your taverna." Nearly three weeks
I've been workin' there now. I get on well with the
customers. Even the Dougies and Jeanettes, we get
a pair of them every week, y'know. They come in,
order a drink an' look all dead nervous at the
menu. I always say to them, "Would you like me
to do y' chips an' egg?" An' they're made up then.
Bein' a part of it here, a proper part of it, it's much
better than bein' on holiday. (*She moves to the
table and puts up the parasol.*) I have most of the
days to meself an' just work the nights. I've got
the night off tonight though. Well, Joe's arrivin'
tonight. The first time he phoned, y'know after
Jane had got back, he screamed at me. He said I
must have finally gone mad. He said I was a
disgrace--to the kids, to him, to meself. It was the
easiest thing in the world to just put the phone
down on him. The second time he phoned he said
you can't run away from life. I said I agreed with
him an' now I'd found some life I had no
intention of runnin' away from it. He started to
scream an' shout again. Then he said he knew
all about me 'holiday romance', an' how I'd made
a fool of meself but--but if I stopped all this arsin'
round, if I got meself on a plane an' got meself
home, where I belonged, he said, he said he'd
promise never to mention it. I said--said..."The

only holiday romance I've had is with meself,
Joe. An'--an' I think...I've come to like meself,
really." I said to him, I said, "I think I'm all
right, Joe. I think that if--if I saw me, I'd say that
woman's   OK...She's   alive.   She's   not
remarkable, she's not gonna--gonna be there in
the history books. But she's--she's there in the
time she' livin' in. An' certainly she's got her
wounds...and   her   battle-scars   but   maybe--
maybe...a little bit of the bull-shit is true an'--an'
the wounds shouldn't be hidden away ...because--
because even the wounds an' the scars are about
bein' alive." There was a long pause. I thought
he'd gone off the phone. An' then I heard this
voice, "I knew it," he was sayin', "I knew it, it's
the bleedin' change of life, isn't it?" "That's
right, Joe," I said, "that's right, it's a change of
life. An' that's why you're wastin' your money
phonin' me to try an' get me back. I'm not comin'
back." The last time he phoned he said our Brian
had been arrested--buskin' without a license. An'
our Millandra was frettin' for me. An' that he
loved me an' the only thing he wanted in the
world was for me to come back. I explained to him
that it was impossible because the woman he
wanted to go back didn't exist anymore. An' then
I got his letter sayin' he was comin' to get me. To
take me back home. Ah, God love him, he must've
been watchin' *Rambo*. He'll be here soon. I hope
he stays for a while. He needs a holiday. He needs
to feel the sun on his skin an' to be in water that's

as deep as forever, an' to have his wet head kissed. He needs to stare out to sea. And to understand. (*pause*) I asked Costas if he'd put the table out for me again. He said to me, "You look for you dream again?" "No, Costas, " I said. "No dream. But I'm gonna sit here an' watch for Joe an' as he walks down the esplanade, an' keeps walkin' because he doesn't recognize me anymore, I'll call out to him. An', as he walks back, an' looks at me, all puzzled and quizzical, I'll say to him, "Hello. I used to be the mother. I used to be the wife. But now, I'm Shirley Valentine again. Would you like to join me for a drink?" (*Blackout*)

Curtain

Costume List

Act One Scene One:

    2 white sweaters
    1 blue printed skirt
    1 pair blue shoes
    1 white belt
    1 pair navy blue tights
    1 pair costume jewelry earrings

Act One Scene Two:

    1 navy blue skirt
    1 white blouse
    1 light blue jacket
    1 white hat
    1 pair blue shoes
    1 pair conservative earrings

Act Two:

    1 pair of casual blue/green trousers
    1 blue/green bikini top
    1 pair blue canvas shoes
    2 head scarves (twisted to make headband)
    1 blue lightweight over-shirt

Working Props

Act I - Scene 1:

- 2 rubberized-plastic placemats, oval with flower design
- 1 bottle of wine, Reisling, 1/3 full
- 1 wine glass, 1/2 full
- 1 bottle stopper
- 1 round plastic wash-up bowl
- 2 tea towels
- 1 wash cloth
- 1 Blue handbag
     w/ Airline tickets
          Perfume atomizer
          Passport
          Drachmas
- 2 tea cups with saucers, white
  6 8 small peeling potatoes
- 1 cutting board
- 1 paring knife
- 2 dinner plates, plain design
- 2 bread plates, to match dinner plates
- 2 dinner knives
- 2 folks
- 2 6-packs of beer
- 6 eggs, raw
- 2 tubs of soft butter
- 1 bread bin
     w/ 6 slices of bread in plain white wrapper
          bread board
          butter knife
- 1 pot with 1/2 chip basket, 17 false chips, covered with lid
- 1 egg slicer (spatula)
- 1 set of salt & pepper shakers
- 1 bottle of steak sauce
- 1 bottle of cooking oil, 1/2 full
- 1 frying pan

Furniture:

- 1 rectangular kitchen table, wood, painted white

-4 armless, seat-padded white chairs to match table
- Outfitted kitchen
    w/ small washing machine
      4 burner stove and oven
      overhead cabinets, and counter space
      double stainless steel sink

Act I-Scene 2:

- 1 white tea cup and saucer
- 1 white porcelain tea pot with hot tea
-1 wash cloth
-1 check list
-1 blue handbag
    w/Airline tickets
      Perfume atomizer
      Passport
      Drachmas
-1 Blue suitcase
-1 "In-flight" bag
    w/ Gillian's blue silk robe
-1 tea towel
-1 egg slicer (spatula)
-1 wall-mounted, small mirror (DL)

Furniture:

- Same as Act I - Scene 1

Act II

-1 bottle of mineral water with cork stopper, 3/4 full
-1 straw bag
    w/ towel
      straw hat
      suntan lotion
-1 paperback book
-1 magazine
-1 pair sunglasses
-1 straw rush matting

-1 sea sponge, dried

Furniture:

- small round outdoor table, tan
- small wicker chair, lt. blue
- sun umbrella, lt. blue (fits into hole in table)

Prop   Preset

Act I - Scene 1:

(Working from DL around kitchen)

LOWER CUPBOARD
        R 6-8 small peeling potatoes in vegetable rack on door
        L 2 dinner plates
          2 bread plates

COUNTER TOP DL
- DS of washing machine--2 cups with saucers (milk in cups to cover bottom)
- Over washing machine--cutting board with knife
- US of washing machine--blue hand bag with contents

SINK
- USL side--damp wash cloth
-. In sink DS--round plastic wash-up bowl with water covering bottom
- Sink divider--crumpled tea towel

HAMPER
- Top upside down with crumpled towels piled in

REFRIDGERATOR
- On freezer door--R list; C pen with magnet; L blank pad
- In freezer--foil-wrapped frozen foods, varied shapes nearly over-flowing freezer

-On fridge door--6 eggs, raw, in carrier
- Top shelf of fridge--2) 6-packs of beer, 1 can loose
- Bottom shelf of fridge--2 tubs of soft butter
Note: Dress balance of fridge with assorted container, food, etc.

COUNTER TOP SR
- US--bread bin with bread, butter knife, bread board
- DS--egg slicer (spatula) on tea towel, upside down 1/2 bottle of cooking oil

OVERHEAD CABINET SR
- US--steak sauce
        salt & pepper shakers

STOVE
- Rear right burner--pot with chip basket, false chips, lid on
- Front left burner--frying pan with oil covering bottom
Note: Check to see that stove is on.

TABLE
- UL Seating--placemat
- DR Seating--placemat
- US--wine bottle 1/3 full; stopper by bottle
- DSR--wine glass 1/2 full

OFF STAGE RIGHT BEHIND SET WALL
- Suitcase & in-flight bag w/blue silk robe packed
- Scene 2 white hat w/check list
- Prop man's strike pan ·

NOTE: All chairs tucked in except DSL, it should be opened up to audience

Act I - Scene 2:

SEE SCENE CHANGES NOTES FROM I-1 to I-2

Act II:

UC POOL OF WATER

- small amount of water in pool, enough to splash, but not to top
-US--mineral water bottle tucked in crevice, 3/4 full

TABLE DL/US OF FLIPPER

- open magazine
- paperback book
- sunglasses
- sea sponge

ROCK LEDGE SL

- straw bag

        w/ towel, straw hat, suntan lotion
- umbrella tucked in crevice US of chair, SR of ledge between ledge and
table

UC ROCK LEDGE

- dressed with crumpled coke can,cigarette package, assorted paper

Prop Scene Change - I-1 to I-2

STRIKE:

From table
- 2 cups and saucers
- 2 placemats
- 1 plate of egg & chips
- 2 bread plates with bread
- 1 bread board and butter knife
- 2 knives & forks
- 1 bottle of wine
- 1 wine glass
- 1 bottle stopper

From DSR
- chopping board and paring knife
- plate from stove

SET:

On table

- 1 teacup w 1/2 milky tea; blue handbag from washer; check list under handbag

On USL chair
- Shirley's white hat

By DSL chair
- suitcase
- In-flight bag

On counter SR
- tea pot with hot tea in it

In fridge
- 1 can of beer

Into oven
- chip pot
- frying pan

Into SR overhead cupboard
- 1 set of salt & pepper shakers
- 1 bottle steak sauce

NOTE: All chairs around table tucked in; close bread bin with butter and bread wrapper in it; turn over top of hamper to conceal dirty towels inside.

Set Dressing List for Act I (starting at door)

1. Tea Towel
2. Fishing Cat
3. Schoolboy Cat
4. Picture with Fir trees
5. Picture with Swans
6. Large blue china plate
7. Wall bracket with ivy in basket
8. Glass carafe 1/2 full of water
9. Blue watering can (full)
10. Fairy liquid
11. Nocturne Royale air freshner

12. French coffee tin with oval sponge
13. Vaseline hand creme
14. Sprint cream cleaner
15. Plastic window box with silk yellow and white flowers
16. Pile of 3 green glass bowls
17. Octagonal glass bowl
18. Toy blue and white umbrella
19. Milk bottle with ivy and spider plant cuttings
20. Candle
21. "London" tray and small round basket with clothespins/string
22. Shell bowl with bay leaves
23. Calendar (May/June)
24. Postcard of House of Parliament
25. "Coaching Days" Tray
26. Square straw mat with kettle on top
27. Small tow owl
28. Kitchen roll holder with roll
29. Square straw mat with tall round wooden tin on it
30. White oval plate
31. Black and white bowl
32. Busy lizzy plant in green pot
33. 2 octagonal glass bowls/top one with bay leaves in it
34. 3 octagonal bowls - empty
35. Wooden biscuit box with painted tulips
36. Mug tree with 5 mugs
37. "Indenture" tray with silver mug and matching sugar bowl
38. Mirror
39. Blue/white flowered biscuit tin
40. White plastic planter containing soap box
41. Yellow biscuit tin with red lid
42. Wicker basket with plastic bag containing tissue paper
43. Matching wicker basket
44. Blue/white small thermos flask
45. Moulinex food mixer
46. White plastic planter with plastic attachment
47. Flowery teapot without lid
48. Dirty white pudding basin
49. Plastic sandwich box
50. Large stoneware plate with matching dish
51. Matching dinner plate with smaller bowl
52. Odd stoneware candlestick

53. Glass vase
54. Glass jar bottomless
55. Small plastic sandwich box
56. Demi-john
57. Pair of men's shoes on top pile of magazines
58. China rabbit on top of fridge
59. Small yellow air freshner on top of fridge
60. Windowlene on top of fridge
61. Nocturne air freshner on top of fridge
62. Plastic pot plant on top of fridge
63. Triangular air freshner on top of fridge
64. Real plant in ridged pot on top of fridge
65. Black striped cloth on top of fridge
66. Ironing board (packed separately)
67. Iron box
68. Iron
69. Note pad, stuck to fridge door
70. Thermometer, stuck to fridge door
71. 3 magnetic airplanes, stuck to fridge door
72. Large white plastic tub on top of SR units
73. Plastic pot plant on top of SR units
74. Dead fern in blue/white pot on top of SR units
75. White wicker plant in pot wit yellow plastic lining on top of SR units
76. Real plant in white mesh pot
77. Bread bin
78. Bread board
79. Knife
80. White apron
81. Toaster
82. Square straw mat
83. Two green dishes with adaptor
84. White coffee jug with brown lid
85. Green vinegar bottle
86. Spice in mayonnaise jar
87. Black peppercorns
88. Spice rack
89. Ice-o-mat
90. Measuring jug
91. Flour jar (full)
92. Sugar jar (full)

93. Blue and white tea caddy
94. Yellow mug containing wooden spoon and spatula
95. Glass water jug
96. Fish slice
97. Two tea towels (wardrobe)
98. 1/2 bottle of oil
99. Chip pan with basket
100. Frying pan
101. Cutlery tray containing at least 2 place settings

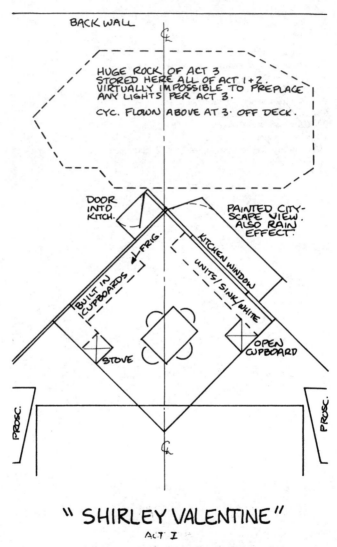

BACK WALL

HUGE ROCK OF ACT 3
STORED HERE ALL OF ACT 1 + 2.
VIRTUALLY IMPOSSIBLE TO PREPLACE
ANY LIGHTS PER ACT 3.

CYC. FLOWN ABOVE AT 3. OFF DECK.

DOOR
INTO
KITCH.

PAINTED CITY-
SCAPE VIEW.
ALSO RAIN
EFFECT.

FRIG.

KITCHEN WINDOW

BUILT IN
CUPBOARDS

UNITS/SINK/WHITE

OPEN
CUPBOARD

STOVE

PROSC.

PROSC.

" SHIRLEY VALENTINE "

ACT I

GROUND PLAN OF KITCHEN

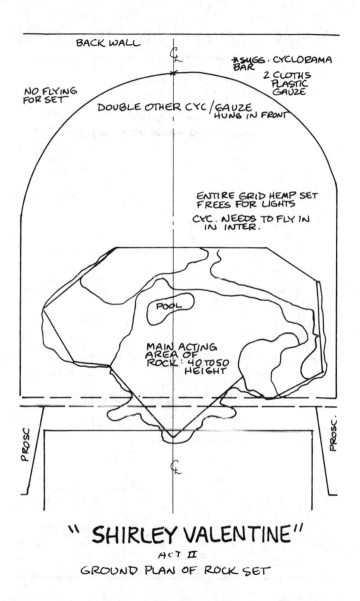

" SHIRLEY VALENTINE "

ACT II
GROUND PLAN OF ROCK SET

Other Publications for Your Interest

TALKING WITH . . .
(LITTLE THEATRE)
By JANE MARTIN

11 women—Bare stage

Here, at last, is the collection of eleven extraordinary monologues for eleven actresses which had them on their feet cheering at the famed Actors Theatre of Louisville—audiences, critics and, yes, even jaded theatre professionals. The mysteriously pseudonymous Jane Martin is truly a "find", a new writer with a wonderfully idiosyncratic style, whose characters alternately amuse, move and frighten us always, however, speaking to us from the depths of their souls. The characters include a baton twirler who has found God through twirling; a fundamentalist snake handler, an ex-rodeo rider crowded out of the life she has cherished by men in 3-piece suits who want her to dress up "like Minnie damn Mouse in a tutu"; an actress willing to go to any length to get a job; and an old woman who claims she once saw a man with "cerebral walrus" walk into a McDonald's and be healed by a Big Mac. "Eleven female monologues, of which half a dozen verge on brilliance."—London Guardian. "Whoever (Jane Martin) is, she's a writer with an original imagination."—Village Voice. "With Jane Martin, the monologue has taken on a new poetic form, intensive in its method and revelatory in its impact."—Philadelphia Inquirer. "A dramatist with an original voice . . . (these are) tales about enthusiasms that become obsessions, eccentric confessionals that levitate with religious symbolism and gladsome humor."—N.Y. Times. *Talking With . . .* is the 1982 winner of the American Theatre Critics Association Award for Best Regional Play. (#22009)

HAROLD AND MAUDE
(ADVANCED GROUPS—COMEDY)
By COLIN HIGGINS

9 men, 8 women—Various settings

Yes: *the Harold and Maude!* This is a stage adaptation of the wonderful movie about the suicidal 19 year-old boy who finally learns how to truly *live* when he meets up with that delightfully whacky octogenarian, Maude. Harold is the proverbial Poor Little Rich Kid. His alienation has caused him to attempt suicide several times, though these attempts are more cries for attention than actual attempts. His peculiar attachment to Maude, whom he meets at a funeral (a mutual passion), is what saves him—and what captivates us. This new stage version, a hit in France directed by the internationally-renowned Jean-Louis Barrault, will certainly delight both afficionados of the film and new-comers to the story. "Offbeat upbeat comedy."—Christian Science Monitor. (#10032)

Other Publications for Your Interest

NOISES OFF
(LITTLE THEATRE—FARCE)
By MICHAEL FRAYN

5 men, 4 women—2 Interiors

This wonderful Broadway smash hit is "a farce about farce, taking the clichés of the genre and shaking them inventively through a series of kaleidoscopic patterns. Never missing a trick, it has as its first act a pastiche of traditional farce; as its second, a contemporary variant on the formula; as its third, an elaborate undermining of it. The play opens with a touring company dress-rehearsing 'Nothing On', a conventional farce. Mixing mockery and homage, Frayn heaps into this play-within-a-play a hilarious melee of stock characters and situations. Caricatures—cheery char, outraged wife and squeaky blonde—stampede in and out of doors. Voices rise and trousers fall . . . a farce that makes you think as well as laugh."—London Times Literary Supplement. ". . . as side-splitting a farce as I have seen. Ever? *Ever.*"—John Simon, NY Magazine. "The term 'hilarious' must have been coined in the expectation that something on the order of this farce-within-a-farce would eventually come along to justify it."—N.Y. Daily News. "Pure fun."—N.Y. Post. "A joyous and loving reminder that the theatre really does go on, even when the show falls apart."—N.Y. Times.   (#16052)

THE REAL THING
(ADVANCED GROUPS—COMEDY)
By TOM STOPPARD

4 men, 3 women—Various settings

The effervescent Mr. Stoppard has never been more intellectually—and *emotionally*—engaging than in this "backstage" comedy about a famous playwright named Henry Boot whose second wife, played on Broadway to great acclaim by Glenn Close (who won the Tony Award), is trying to merge "worthy causes" (generally a euphemism for left-wing politics) with her art as an actress. She has met a "political prisoner" named Brodie who has been jailed for radical thuggery, and who has written an inept play about how property is theft, about how the State stifles the Rights of The Individual, etc., etc., etc. Henry's wife wants him to make the play work theatrically, which he does after much soul-searching. Eventually, though, he is able to convince his wife that Brodie is emphatically *not* a victim of political repression. He is, in fact, a *thug*. Famed British actor Jeremy Irons triumphed in the Broadway production (Tony Award), which was directed to perfection by none other than Mike Nichols (Tony Award). "So densely and entertainingly packed with wit, ideas and feelings that one visit just won't do . . . Tom Stoppard's most moving play and the most bracing play anyone has written about love and marriage in years."—N.Y. Times. "Shimmering, dazzling theatre, a play of uncommon wit and intelligence which not only thoroughly delights but challenges and illuminates our lives."—WCBS-TV. 1984 Tony Award-Best Play.   (#941)

Other Publications for Your Interest

BENEFACTORS
(LITTLE THEATRE—COMIC DRAMA)
By MICHAEL FRAYN

2 men, 2 women—Interior

Do not expect another *Noises Off*; here the multi-talented Mr. Frayn has more on his mind than Just Plain Fun. *Benefactors*, a long-running Broadway and London hit, is about doing good and do-gooding (not the same) and about the way the world changes outside your control just when you are trying to change it yourself. The story concerns an architect who has the sixties notion that if you give people good environments they will be good people. But, given a South London development to design, he is forced by town planners to go for a high-rise, characterless scheme. No sooner does he begin to believe in this scheme than the fashion for high rises goes bust. ". . . one of the subtlest plays Broadway has seen in years, by one of the most extraordinary writers of the English-speaking theater . . . more political than most political plays, more intimate than most intimate plays and wiser than almost any play around today."—Newsweek. ". . . a fine . . . very good play . . . A Christmas present for theatergoers."—WABC-TV. ". . . a high point of the theater season . . . rare wit and intelligence."—Wall Street Journal. ". . . fascinating and astonishing play . . ."—N.Y. Daily News. ". . . dazzling and devastating play . . ."—N.Y. Times. ". . . a tour de force . . . simultaneously compelling and alienating . . ."—Christian Science Monitor. (#3980)

PACK OF LIES
(LITTLE THEATRE—DRAMA)
By HUGH WHITEMORE

3 men, 5 women—Combination interior

Bob and Barbara Jackson are a nice middle-aged English couple. Their best friends are their neighbors, Helen and Peter Kroger, who are Canadian. All is blissful in the protected, contained little world of the Jacksons; until, that is, a detective from Scotland Yard asks if his organization may use the Jackson's house as an observation station to try and foil a Soviet spy ring operating in the area. Being Good Citizens the Jacksons oblige, though they become progressively more and more put out as Scotland Yard's demands on them increase. They are really put to the test when the detective reveals to them that the spies are, in fact, their best friends the Krogers. Scotland Yard asks the Jacksons to cooperate with them to trap the spies, which really puts the Jacksons on the horns of a dilemma. Do they have the right to "betray" their friends? "This is a play about the morality of lying, not the theatrics of espionage, and, in Mr. Whitemore's view, lying is a virulent disease that saps patriots and traitors alike of their humanity."—N.Y. Times. "A crackling melodrama."—Wall St. Journal. "Absolutely engrossing . . . an evening of dynamic theatre."—N.Y. Post. "A superior British drama."—Chr. Sci. Mon. (#18154)